T0114972

The Treasures for Ascension from the God of All Knowing

KHAMSONE LIMSAVANH

BALBOA.
PRESS
A DIVISION OF HAY HOUSE

Balboa Press books may be ordered through booksellers or by contacting:

Balboa Press
A Division of Hay House
1663 Liberty Drive
Bloomington, IN 47403
www.balboapress.com
1 (877) 407-4847

Because of the dynamic nature of the Internet, any web addresses or
links contained in this book may have changed since publication and
may no longer be valid. The views expressed in this work are solely those
of the author and do not necessarily reflect the views of the publisher,
and the publisher hereby disclaims any responsibility for them.

The author of this book does not dispense medical advice or prescribe the use
of any technique as a form of treatment for physical, emotional, or medical
problems without the advice of a physician, either directly or indirectly. The
intent of the author is only to offer information of a general nature to help
you in your quest for emotional and spiritual well-being. In the event you use
any of the information in this book for yourself, which is your constitutional
right, the author and the publisher assume no responsibility for your actions.

Any people depicted in stock imagery provided by Getty Images are
models, and such images are being used for illustrative purposes only.
Certain stock imagery © Getty Images.

Print information available on the last page.

ISBN: 978-1-9822-0033-6 (sc)
ISBN: 978-1-9822-0034-3 (e)

Balboa Press rev. date: 03/13/2018

I dedicate this book to the woman I love and the people in Cambodia who help protect and preserve the ancient carving of the Churning of the World Ocean of Milk in Angkor Wat.

Love,
Khamsone

ACKNOWLEDGMENTS

My thanks go to the two people who made this book possible—Monica N. and Monica Hilbert.

PROLOGUE

The universe has a way of getting people to do whatever it wants. In this case, it used a woman to lure me out from my hiding place.

I am an ascended being, meaning that all the complaints about life most people take for granted are trivial to me. I have achieved the highest—immortal existence. I'm just waiting for my turn to die and leave this prison that others call life and never return.

But a woman who is broken and disturbed beyond understanding infuriates me. She has all the symptoms and signs of depression, and she is possibly possessed. As morbid as it sounds, she agreed to this contract from the other side before this life. This is supposedly her last life reincarnation if she can pull it off. However, I am compelled to help her all I can because she is part of this world. My helping her means helping the entire world she is.

I must reveal to the world the way of ascension and of myself. After consulting with friends, I have decided to write a book about my life as an ascended being. Writing is not my strong suit; it was not even when I was in college. But now, it's a necessary tool to convey messages to the world.

While I was in the thick of writing this book, something

peculiar about my writing didn't fit with my method of operation. I cannot explain where some of the ideas in my writing came from. Each time I completed a paragraph, I would go back to the beginning and read it aloud. To my astonishment, the writing itself was teaching and enlightening me as if someone else were writing it and using me as just a tool. Baffled by this enigma, I tried consulting my good friend Monica Hilbert, a gifted psychic.

She told me that as I wrote, I was channeling the god of all knowing, a supreme being I had encountered in a vision long ago. He terrified me, and I was scared out of my wits to learn that this omnipotent being was still with me after all these years of coaching me and guiding my hands. I hated to fail him by not delivering his divine messages to the world. I do not want to sound callous, but I think people are very fortunate to have learned and hopefully have assimilated the messages of deliverance from the god of logic. He must have a plan. After all, he is the god of all knowing.

CHAPTER 1

The Island of Vessel

The Boat Builders

The first boat builder was a young, androgynous prince who had the patience of a turtle. One day, he was sent to the Island of Vessel by the gods, and he wandered the island for a long time. When he finally realized the island was an eternal prison for his soul, getting out became his priority. It took him a long time, but he built a boat. A boat with no oar. A magical boat that could ferry him off the prison island and into reality. He was the Lord Buddha. The rest is history.

Centuries later, another boat builder was sent to the island. He was a carpenter from Nazareth, the son of the Virgin Mary. He woke up alone in a place that looked very different from his homeland. He set out to explore the island for any sign of life to assist him, but he found no one, and there was no sign of life.

Scared and alone, the carpenter broke down in tears, fell to his knees, and cried in despair as if he were trapped in a nightmare. After a while, he grew tired and wandered off in his thoughts. Sometime later, he started to summon his strength and held his head high. He looked for a sign, and then he cried out, "Why have thou forsaken me?"

What seemed to be great despair turned into a deep prayer with all humility and devotion. Then came a long silence. His inner voice was becoming louder. It was the voice of God, which filled him with hope and joy. The carpenter heeded the voice. Great jubilation followed. The carpenter armed himself with this new revelation and without hesitation started to build a boat with no oar. Jesus Christ was the second boat builder. The rest is biblical history.

Last Resort

The gods had seen enough and wanted to start the next phase of human evolution. After discussing the matter, they decided to send another boat builder, one who was no prince of men and who had no trade or skills. From an obscure life came a young man from Laos.

Arriving on the island when he was gullible and young, the refugee from Laos woke up alone in a beautiful and peaceful place. Vegetation and trees stretched far beyond what he could see. The radiant morning sun shone on the still, crystal-clear water and illuminated the lush meadows and scenery. It seemed that the lakes and basins had been collecting rainwater from the night before.

This must be paradise, the young man thought. He reminisced about the time when he had to endure the ordeals of being a refugee. But at last, on the island, he was experiencing a welcomed change—and relief.

Hours passed as the young man lay there enjoying this beautiful paradise—or so it seemed. Like most young men, he just wanted to be left alone and bask in the quiet morning sun. But the quiet suddenly turned to dead silence. *Too quiet*, the young man thought. He woke from his stupor and realized the quiet was surreal. All his senses were on high alert trying to detect anything no matter how small or faint. But there was nothing—no birds were chirping, no wind was blowing, and no sound of life was anywhere. Realizing he was alone, he panicked.

He set out eastward through meadows and pastures and past more trees and ponds. He noticed something peculiar about the sun—hours had gone by since he had arrived, but it had never changed position. It seemed to maintain the same spot in the sky. As he kept moving, he noticed there were no flowers anywhere, no bees, and no insects.

Overwhelmed by the endless oddities of the place, the young man kept on moving until he arrived at a sandy beach. There, more oddities awaited him. The beaches were surrounded by an unusually calm ocean; again—no waves, no ebb or flow of tides. Hovering over the sea was a strange fog that engulfed the beach and obscured the view beyond. His only option was to head back.

On his way back, he came upon the surrounding in which he had awoken the first time. He pondered the matter for a moment but then kept moving in the opposite direction from his starting point and picked up the pace.

Sometime later, he reached the other side of the island—a beach with the same weirdness as the other. Frustrated and confused, he ran back and forth in all directions always finding more beaches in the end. Stumbling around aimlessly like a person who was about to give up, he ended up back where he had started. He tried to comprehend the sheer madness and bizarreness of this place. Exhausted by the whole experience, he managed to make some sense and a thought came to his mind—*Island*.

The Island

"An island? But How? Why?" he cried out. He ranted and raved. He was tormented by his memories. He had grown up in a country ravaged by a devastating war that seemed to have no end. He had lost everything in that senseless war. Penniless and stripped of all human dignity, he was confined on this weird and uninhabited island for an unknown reason. With no loved ones to console him, no warm place to call home, and no country to be part of, his existence was next to nothing. He was nothing. But he had a will to live, and that meant he must escape that place.

First, he assessed his surroundings. Despite being simpleminded and young, he could comprehend his situation. He could tell he was not on earth; rather, he was somewhere off-world. Or maybe in another universe. In spite of the strangeness of his locale, he could manipulate his surrounding forces and energy with his mind. He could levitate and fly around like Peter Pan, and sometimes, he could move objects at will.

With these new, strange abilities, he took off from the sandy beach and flew east into the strange fog. Staying just above water, he glided in the mist for about fifteen minutes before he grew tired and crashed into the water. He drowned only to wake up again back on the island.

He tried rafting and then swimming across the sea, but those attempts also resulted in his drowning and again coming back to life on the island. He saw no way out. He felt nothing but despair and frustration, so he turned his attention toward his creator. With rage and anger as his allies, he had the audacity to call on God and the universe to let him know why he was there. There was no answer. No sign of anything. He persisted until he could no longer maintain his sanity.

But when one's mind is pushed beyond the edge of oblivion, something extraordinary happens. His body was consumed by rage and anger. He shouted at the empty sky, "What do you want from me?" He looked and listened for any response, but there was nothing. His mind had drifted to a point of no return. "All right! All right! I have nothing left anymore of my life, of my family—nothing!" But again, there was no response.

He reluctantly accepted his fate; he would be alone. His mind and spirit began capitulating to his fate. Childhood fears started surfacing including the fear of being alone. The thought of not being wanted or needed was his cruel fate, a fate far worse than death, filled his mind. He felt the chilling cold in his lonely heart as if his soul had broken to pieces and vanished. "Feels like I'm dying," he whispered. He was cold and alone. He was drifting slowly toward oblivion, but suddenly and miraculously, he heard a warm, angelic voice call out to him from the depth of his fragmented soul. It was from her.

The Reason to Live

"Don't be afraid. You're not alone," she whispered softly. Like a phoenix rising from ashes, he stood. As if by instinct and for the first time in his meek existence, he wanted to live, to love, and to be with her. He felt energized as if no cage could hold him—and certainly not an island. Being with her was the only thought on his mind. But first, he would need to escape that cursed island by any means. Empowered by the miraculous feelings of desire, he grew restless and furious at being stuck there when instead he should have been off searching for her, the only person who meant the world to him.

After a while, reality started to sink in, and to his consternation, he thought there was no escaping the island. He struggled to understand what crime he had committed to have been sent there. He felt with all certainty that he had committed no crime that could justify his being imprisoned there. He became more angry, frustrated, and rebellious. He was like a man possessed when he shouted, "All right! If nothingness is what you want me to be, then let me return the favor! How about I turn this whole damn island into nothing?"

In defiance, he fiercely extended his arms to the side with palms out. With the power of rage and anger gathering on his palms, he was able to warp time and space on each side and simultaneously generate two event singularities—small black holes.

As the two singularities reached critical mass, he tried to implode them with his remaining energy. Two fireballs appeared and absorbed the two singularities in the blink of an eye. Gone. Only the two fireballs remained. They were the gods.

Destruction and Logic

Suspended in midair, the fireballs positioned themselves around him as if to contain him. They were the size of bowling balls but burned red hot with flames. They hovered near him as if they were judges, juries, and maybe executioners. No mistake—these were very powerful beings. Angry faces appeared in the fireball to his left and screamed and growled with rage and anger. In the fireball to his right, an emotionless face appeared and seemed almost mechanical but just as powerful.

With disregard for his own life, he approached the fireball on his left, but it was too dangerous. The awesome power and rage emanating from the faces were too intense. Fearing for his life, he stepped back, collected himself, and turned to his right. To run was unthinkable. There was no safe place to run to, and he had come too far and had committed possibly the worst sin since the time of Garden of Eden maybe.

With no other option, he approached the being on the right and came face to face with the god of logic, the god of all knowing. He was frozen in place by the awesome power of the god. He was helpless, unable to do anything. He stared intensely into his own death by the awesome flame that he was sure would incinerate him.

The seconds that went by were an eternity to him. He experienced flashes of visions of all his reincarnations—his past, present, and futures selves—colliding and collapsing into one. And with that, humanity itself manifested to him and compelled him to ask questions of the god of all knowing.

Three Questions, Three Answers

"What is the meaning of life?" he asked naively. Without much reservation, the emotionless god started speaking in Aramaic intending to be understood only by his Semitic-speaking incarnations and certainly not addressing the young man's present form. For some unknown reason, he was satisfied with the answer though he did not entirely understand it.

"Why are we here?" the young man asked referring to earth. Again, the god replied in Aramaic, and again, the young man was satisfied with the answer.

"How do I get off this island?" the young man asked impatiently. The god of logic urged him to look to his right; three trees appeared out of nowhere. The tree in the middle was bigger and taller than the other two, but it had been dead for a long time. In plain English but in the manner of a riddle, the god of logic said, "Cut down these trees, and build a boat with them. Use planks from the tree on the left to make the left side of the boat. Use planks from the tree on the right to make the right side of the boat. Use planks from the dead tree to make the keel of the boat. This boat will take you from this island."

Satisfied with the answers, the young man stepped away slowly not knowing that the god of all knowing was looking at him and was concerned that the messages might not reach humanity in time or maybe not at all. The young refugee from Laos was Khamsone.

CHAPTER 2

My Life Path

I was born in Laos in a simple, makeshift shelter among livestock early on a Wednesday morning in 1967. The creation of something extraordinary was in the making. According to some relatives, the night had been eerily dark as if darkness itself descending upon the village. No one could see anything even with the help of torches and flashlights.

When I let out my first cry, most of the people and even my grandfather ran off in fear. Only a midwife and a handful of brave women stayed to help my mother.

I was born on the last day of the year of the Fire Horse; it foretold portentous calamities and misfortunes to those dear to me. Great sacrifices had to be made with the blood of my family to draw the secrets from the world beyond.

In 1975, Laos went through major changes in governments, ideologies, and some new ways of living all of which were not suitable for my family. We were closely affiliated with the old regime, and that complicated things for us.

In 1979, my family decided they had enough and escaped to Thailand to find a new life anywhere but Laos. In Thailand, we established ourselves as refugees and lived at first in a refugee camp. We left everything in the hands of fate, and fate fortunately delivered us to the land of promise, the land of the free—America with its many blessings.

For me, America was and still is the land of many firsts for me—my first alphabet, my first taste of freedom, my first experience of electricity and its applications. It was the land that produced the first aviators and the first to walk on the moon. These were all good things about America, but there were and are dark sides to America as well. It invented the atomic bomb and was the first to use it on human beings. If almighty God ever set foot on earth, it would be in America.

Why Me?

On many occasions, I've asked myself, *Why not someone else like a Harvard grad?* But the gods had chosen me. By all appearances, I am nothing special. I have no higher education. I'm frugal by nature and necessity. I'm a loner. My freedom is everything to me, but my take on life is a different story. Figuratively speaking, I am no less than a titan but no greater than a dying star. Too much? Joking aside, I am the vessel for secrets and knowledge from the world beyond chosen by omnipotent and omniscient interdimensional beings.

Why Ascension?

The singular purpose of all life forms in existence—physical or energy in all realities and dimensions of all the universes—is to ascend to greater heights. Our soul matrices are the sparks encoded with the original program of the source, our creator, God. Therefore, don't let any fool tell you that you are nobody and that you can't aspire to anything in this world. Karma is not a punishment but a challenge to gain experiences and eventually evolve higher as individuals. In this world, there is no limit to anyone's potential. We are all gods in the lowest forms and have nowhere to go but up. Before you ever strike anyone, realize you are about to inflict harm on a god.

What Is Ascension?

Lord Buddha would be best one to explain everything about ascension. With love and respects to Buddha, he'll probably say that job is for someone else—me. So, you're stuck with me. I have ascended trice already, but I'm still no expert on ascension. Perhaps ascension is uniquely different for others. I don't remember my first; the unique thing about it was that my physical body ascended also. Possibly, ascension didn't imply just my soul but my physical body as well.

Sadly, the process of ascension means the soul must leave the body and go to a higher plane of existence, and sometimes, that results in instant death. By comparison, in the soul level between sleep and ascension, in the state of sleep, one is somewhat dying but the soul is still chained to the body; whereas in ascension, the soul will leave the body completely unchained.

Depending on the meditation practices, the plane of existence levels one ascends, and the higher level of ascension, the more infused energy and vibrations the soul will experience and the longer it will take. Make no mistake—the process or experience of ascension is the same as dying. Worst case, the soul does not return to the body in time, and eventually, the body withers and dies.

Path to Ascension

I got home late from a bad poker night angry and confused. I prepared myself for my usual meditation session. Having cleansed myself with smoke from purified incense, I sat on my chair crossed-legged and looked out a window of my two-story house in Holland, Michigan. I used a pillow to support my back. I faced south as always.

I started meditating when I was in the US Army. It was a way to calm myself after the daily challenges of army life. After the army, I continued perfecting my technique of meditation for twelve years until that night, a cool and calm October night, a perfect night for any occasion.

I slowly breathed in and out to calm myself for about five minutes. I then carefully balanced my logic and emotions on a horizontal bar. I called upon a higher power or God for cleansing in the form of white light from the Holy Spirit surrounding me and protecting me from all that was dark and negative. (That stage is very delicate and important if you want to avoid possession; it is not recommended for weaker personae.)

I stayed relaxed, calmed my breathing further, and let go of everything I perceived as life. For me, summoning energy from nature is as simple as thinking it and it would surround me and course through me much like dragon or kundalini energy.

In forty-five minutes, I was in a deep state of meditation and no longer attached to the world of man. At that point, I normally stayed relaxed and listened in with the universe, but not that night. I needed to go beyond the barrier, push beyond my limitations, and experience the true essence of ascension. *What is holding me back?* I wondered. *Why am I still so heavy?* After a long pulse—*Eureka!* I knew what I had to do.

The Awakening

My body started acting on its own to compensate for whatever drastic or extraordinary thing was about to take place. I was breathing heavily and taking in more air than usual. My body started stiffening. Like a pilot listening for the results of final checks before taking off, I waited for my body to give me the green light to finally let go of whatever was holding me back. When it happened, I instinctively recited, "I am the might of God!"

Immediately, my third eye opened and I saw my left and right eyes merging into one in the middle as one complete soul. I shot straight up into the ether leaving my body behind. There I was surrounded by a white light and merging into my real body, the sun. I was complete. I was full. I was existence itself. I was the universe. I was a god.

Five minutes later, an interruption brought me back

down to my human body. When I came to, I was aware that the only thing powerful enough to pull me out of my ascension was destiny. Apparently, it was not done with me.

The US Army

In late 1992, I joined the US Army. I was twenty-four, and I had many issues and a personal agenda I needed to resolve. I attended boot camp in Fort Benning, Georgia, home of the infantry. This boot camp was harder than the one in the movie *Full Metal Jacket*. I gave everything I had but barely made it. Not many were successful, but those who were ended up crying and broken down in tears at the end. It was an emotional and grueling journey. For some, the war had ended, but for others including myself, the war had just begun. I faced three long and excruciating years.

After boot camp, I joined the Third Platoon Wolfpack of Alpha Company of the First Battalion of the 87th Infantry of the First Brigade of the Tenth Mountain Division in Fort Drum, New York. I was five six and weighed one hundred and sixty pounds. I was the perfect killing machine Uncle Sam wanted. *Hurrah!*

Death

My greatest teacher and mentor, the deity I held in high regard, was Lord Death. Dressed in an all-black uniform and with full insignias and decorations, Lord Death approached me in the form of a colonel and made himself known to me.

I bowed in respect and paid homage to him by offering him some coins. He responded in kind words.

The cemetery was his office, his power base. The tombstones were in his throne room, where he presided over the kingdom of the dead. He had taken my entire family just to show me the value of life and loneliness. Of all the lessons of death, none was more profound and spiritual than the one I had when I was drowning.

It happened when I was nine. I was swimming alone in the calm Nam Se River in Laos. Though I considered myself a strong swimmer, I was careful not to venture beyond the edge of safety, past an underwater cliff that dropped straight to the bottom. That was my daily activity to keep myself cool and clean. And it was fun to play in the water. But on that fateful day, I swam a little farther out, just beyond the safety. I was alone. Then it happened.

The water came alive and took me under and straight to the bottom. But I didn't go down easily. I struggled and fought back hard, but the water was in its element, and my struggles were in vain. On my way down to meet my maker, I choked on water. It flooded my lungs. I was paralyzed. Only my sight was working. I saw the light growing dimmer as I descended into the abyss. I reached bottom. It was completely dark. I lost consciousness.

Sometime later, I regained consciousness, but barely. I started to see the light again. It was getting brighter and brighter. I thought, *This must be the afterlife. I'm ascending to heaven.* No, that wasn't it. I was very much alive but still underwater. *How can I still be alive?* The same water that had been trying to drown me moments ago was trying to save me by pushing me to the surface and onto the safety of a rock. It rested my helpless body on it and vanished.

I coughed and expelled water for agonizing minutes. I cried my eyes out. When I started breathing normally again, I regained feeling in my body. I stood and walked, but I was weak from the ordeal. I quickly gathered my things and ran like the devil from there. I never looked back. I wanted to stay far away from that place forever.

The Moon

According to astrology, the moon is considered a planet or a planet moon. According to duality, the moon is considered a place for the dead just as the earth is considered a place for the living. In many respects, the moon affects our minds and our emotional states. When the moon is full, its effects are intensified to the point that many ascensions take place. For those seeking ascension, it's crucial that meditation be the only activity or inactivity during a full moon.

Aliens?

Many strange incidents happened to me during my teen years. One involved the moon. One night, I was asleep in my room but was awakened. I looked out my window and saw the full moon. As I gazed at it, I saw a sparkling, shining light next to the moon spinning around the moon. As the spinning became more intense, the moon transformed into a gateway that tried to suck my soul out of my body. A flash of white light cut between me and the moon, and I fell back into my body. I experienced a sharp, excruciating pain in my chest and all over my body. I spent hours crying myself to sleep. Days went by, and all the while, I hated the moon for what it had done to me.

Many years later, I asked the gods about that incident. They told me that the moon was innocent, that aliens had tried to extract my energy in their quest for knowledge about ascensions. The gods told me that advanced alien beings had visited earth long ago and had put something on the moon that acted as a detector and amplifier of unique energy signatures such as mine. They wanted to extract it and take it to their home planet using the moon as camouflage.

Extracting energy my eye! I was sure they had been trying to kill me and steal my soul. Had my protective angels not put a stop to that, I would have been dead. I had no idea how many souls had been taken or how long that had been going on. One thing for sure—they're still doing it.

Witches and Demons

My energy signature is unique by design. Witches and demons are drawn to my energy much like moths to a flame. The gods use me to draw out these elusive demons who find me so irresistible that they want to devour me.

The gods want to create a new agenda by cleansing certain parts of the world of demons, and they use any means necessary including using me as bait. But witches are a different story because they are humans. As such, they fall under the aegis of human laws, so they are not influenced by otherworldly forces, at least not directly.

Witches are by and large are good people who can tap into the forces of nature and use them to cast spells and other miracles to help us with healing, fertility, good harvests, and good fortunes, read our futures, and protect us from harm among other things. The downside of that is that some witches are parasitic; they tap into the wrong sources—other human psyches—or worse, the dark side. They can become addicted to these activities so much that when they die, they turn into succubi or incubi—demons that assail you from the outside or the inside respectively. That's bad.

Succubi

From my teen years until I was thirty-seven, I was possessed by a succubus, a shadowy, shape-shifting demon capable of transforming into any shape or form. It started during my pubescent years. One night, I woke up to find a pitch-dark, shadowy figure floating at the edge of my bed. I was paralyzed. I could not move or speak. It was as if this thing were trying to take total control of me. Fear and unspeakable evil were emanating from this abomination. I tried hard to stay awake, but my fear was overwhelming. I passed out.

When I came to the next morning, I felt tired and dirty as if a part of me was no longer innocent. At first, I thought it had been a nightmare that every teenager had to go through, but those nightly visits became more frequent, interactive, and perverse. Some nights, I was too scared to fall asleep. And when I came to the next morning, I was too embarrassed to tell anyone let alone believe that my nightmares had happened.

This thing was cunning, insidious, perverse, and powerful as if it were guided by a superior intelligence. It knew what it was doing. It latched onto my soul as if it were a shadow feeding on my energy like a parasite. It haunted me at night, and during the day, it whispered perversions to my better conscience. I had to struggle just to make a simple moral decision. I felt my soul slipping further and further into the abyss.

During my time in the army, this thing thrived on my pain and suffering by indulging itself to the point that it didn't need to make any nocturnal visits; it drank its fill in the daytime. But after my time in the army, it was back as usual and sometimes two to three times a week. It was affecting me so badly that I had to drop out of school. I became antisocial and estranged from my family and friends. I was traumatized by this thing for many years. When I got tired of feeling scared all the time, I fought back.

I became immune to its dark power, and I was able to stay awake and move at will enough to defend myself. Maybe I was crazy or something, but one night, I managed to take a bite out of its face, and it screamed in agony like a wounded animal. It then vanished.

I knew it would return in a few weeks; I prepared myself for that. I researched how to get rid of it, but unfortunately, there was no cure, no miracle, no spell. I had no hope of getting rid of this thing. I felt that the gods knew about it and didn't want to deal with it no matter how hard or how many times I prayed to them.

They probably thought that if it couldn't kill me, it

would make me stronger. That may be the case, but I didn't want to be strong like it, like a demon; I just wanted to be free from it. Also, I'd learned that back in the Vatican's early history, a revered pope confessed on his deathbed that he was possessed by a demon called a succubus. Even a pope who prayed earnestly to God was not exempt from possession.

As the years went on, I became stronger and even able to anticipate when the next visit would take place. Sleeping allows most people's bodies to heal, but for me, going to bed meant I had to prepare myself for battle with a creature of the night for the sake of my soul. Yes, there was a cure, a miracle cure indeed. I found it. But it came with price, the highest price of all—ascension.

Rise of the Goddesses

In the past, most prosperous and enduring dynasties were ruled by extraordinary women, from a pharaoh of ancient Egyptian to the great Queen of Sheba and Queen Elizabeth I. These exceptional women did not let religion or tradition stop them from accomplishing their goals. They personified their true goddess natures.

In today's political world, we call on them again to be our salvation, our future leaders who will lead us to a better world filled with everlasting peace and harmony. I love and respect them dearly.

I think that long ago, the gods took pity on man and disguised their daughters as ordinary women—mothers, sisters, and faithful companions to man. They were gifts from the gods. We have asked too much of them already, but they haven't begun to explore their potential.

I speak to them directly and say you can operate both sides of your brain any time and stay beautiful even when you're crying and soaked in tears. Just imagine the day that you can tap into your true goddess potential—the sooner the better. There is no telling what you can do.

Please, wake up from this trance that man put you under long ago and save us from these half-brained, corrupt, egotistical, warmongering men who will destroy us and our future again. You must rise, take your rightful place in our futures, and lead us beyond the stars. There, in tribute to all goddesses, a sacred banner of peace and hope will be flown among and beyond the edge of creation. You must stay true and believe in yourself and your destinies. I probably won't live to see it, but I'll pray for that day.

War

As newly ascended being, I am occasionally tested. The divines are trying to understand me and what I'm capable of by putting my soul back into their plane of existence to see which deity will come for the bait.

Sure enough, the god of war shows up. First, he flies back and forth trying to survey the area around me, and then he vanishes. Moments later, he shows up again, but this time, he is walking. He looks like an ancient Greek god down from Olympus and fully embroidered in flashy and shiny precious gems. But make no mistake—he is a god of war, powerful and domineering.

My instinct tells me to be on high alert. He is waiting

for me to make the first move and to disrespect the gods. Should that happen, he will unleash hell on me. I have but a slim chance of being on par with him, and even that cannot guarantee a favorable outcome. It can go either way. It will all depend on luck.

As luck would have it, the god of war makes the first move and challenges me one on one. He is not known for his patience; that works to my advantage. It gives me a small fighting chance because he has shown his vanity. When gods do that, they lose some of their powers. Nonetheless, he is still a force to be reckoned with.

Reluctantly, I accept his challenge. To turn down a challenge from a god would be unthinkable. He challenges me out of respect for me; he is acknowledging me as his equal. I don't know what will be the outcome. All know is that I'm in big trouble.

He pulls out a bullwhip, his preferred weapon. I have no weapon but my hands. He's not fighting fair. There will not be any fighting; I will just take a beating from the god of war.

His first strike with the whip knocks me off my feet and into the air. I land on my back and in such pain that I want to stay there. *What happened? What hit me?* The god of war is taunting me and telling me to stay down and admit defeat. He mocks me. I have had enough. Despite my pain, I want to kill that son of a bitch.

I slowly get back up. If not for my experience with ascension, I would be in serious pain. I'm thinking about how I will counter his attacks. He is standing a hundred feet away beyond my reach, but he still manages to land blows on me again and again with his whip. I don't know how I keep getting back up. Maybe I'm too stupid to feel pain.

He whips me; I feel blow after blow at a consistent pace. Feeling confident and complacent, he continues his onslaught with ease. I have no respect for him and his stature as a god. In fact, I despise him. For that reason, I know I can defeat him.

But his blows are relentless. Each feels more powerful than the last. They are so powerful that they create a big crater all around me, and I'm standing knee deep in it. I have dirt all over me—on my hands, in my mouth, and everywhere else. Upon seeing me covered with dirt, he laughs at me and carefully takes aim at me. But this time, I catch the weapon of the god of war.

The dirt on my hands neutralizes the power of the whip and renders it useless. Realizing my good fortune, I yank it from his hands, reel it in, and bury it knowing that will ground his divine powers.

With no weapon, the god of war is in dismay and bewildered. I jump at him and knock him off his feet. He lands on his back. I punch his godly face. I want to punch him some more, but he is already knocked out. I know the other gods are watching, and I don't want them to feel sympathy for him. I walk away feeling satisfied and relieved.

Later, he approaches me and badgers me about my victory. He thinks it's impossible for me to have defeated him. I humbly explain that luck was simply on my side. The god of war takes a last look at me, and then he is gone.

The god of war can be defeated. That means that war is losing its power over humanity and that peace on earth will become reality someday soon.

Back to the Island

When I came face to face with the terrifying beings on the island, I learned many secrets from them—secrets they wanted me to convey to humanity. But before that could happen, I had to pass a test to be worthy of such a divine gift. Supposedly, they'd searched the world for a unique energy signature befitting and worthy of their curiosity. They found me, a perfect test subject for their quest to ascertain whether humanity was ready for what was to come.

The tests were impossible. I died many times during them but was brought back to life each time. I thought the gods were underestimating humanity and were toying with people. Each time I died, I came back stronger. I became so strong that I came close to destroying heaven, or the continuum, or whatever that place was. I thought it was a mistake on their part to allow me to have gotten that far. It took two supreme beings to contain me and subdue my madness; otherwise, I could have extinguished all life perhaps.

We're more than ready and desperately starving for changes in how we view the world and ourselves. The gods wanted someone extreme, a daredevil, someone who could catch a bull by its horns and risk it all when it counted. But that person also had to have a caring, kind, and gentle side that embraced life; that person would have to care for the environment and love humanity.

What Is the Meaning of Life?

All existence is shaped like a pyramid or the great pyramid of existence if you will. The pyramid is the perfect shape in geometry and nature. This pyramid is formed by stacking layers of dimensions or universes on top of one another. We, the lowest dimension form the base, the third dimension. The layers ascend to the apex, a small but perfect pyramid, the first pyramid. It existed before time, before creation, and is the only perfect shape in existence.

Residing in this first pyramid is none other than God himself, the perfect being. As events unfold, the dimension just below the first pyramid is occupied by the final eights. They are the supreme beings, the cardinals of the gods—only eight of them. They handle all major decisions regarding the realities, dimensions, or universes. Not many have heard of them, and the gods and angels refused to divulge any information about them until now.

They represent the eight forces of nature—the eight spokes of the great wheel of Dharma—and their eternal flames are fueled by our passions, desires, curiosities, and so forth. I had the rare privilege of an audience with two of the eight supreme beings, the god of destruction and god of all knowing. Below them are the host of angels or gods, ascended beings, spirit guides, and interdimensional beings.

Finally, we, the third dimension who form the base of the pyramid, are the last in the pyramid of existence. The great pyramid has faces shaped like four perfect triangles extending from the apex to the base. The four great triangles represent the four beliefs, the four great religions of the world that can resonate to the apex. I will leave you to determine which four religions those are.

The first pyramid has five facets or attributes of the perfect object in existence, God. Therefore, five is a divine number. There are five in one in all things that are perfect and in balance in the world. For example, there are five fingers in a hand, five senses in a human being, and so on. There you have it—the meaning of life.

Why Are We Here on Earth?

We are all here to tend the garden of the trio, the garden of the sacred triangle. In this garden are the tree of love, the tree of agony, and the tree of righteousness side by side on the soil of our physical bodies. Our actions and experiences in this world provide nutrients and sustenance necessary to nurture these trees.

The tree of agony is forever contained by the tree of love and the tree of righteous to prevent its negativity from escaping. By design, we are meant to be happy and full of joy in heart and mind, but we're not here on vacation or for a honeymoon; we're here to get right down to the business of becoming stronger.

Sadly, we punish ourselves with challenges imposed on us by design; our bodies are subjected to pain and suffering beyond the ordinary to evolve as souls. Some might call it tough love. In any case, if we want love, we have to get tougher. All the same, our bodies must be allowed time to rest and relax, to enjoy good food and other delight so they can heal.

How Can We Get off the Island of Vessel?

The Island of Vessel is the symbolic body of everyone alive on earth. When the gods test me, they confine me to the island—my body. I am my soul imprisoned on the island of my body. There is but one way off the island, and finding it is part of the test. It is a lot like the legend of the Gordian knot. When I die during my escape attempts but come back to life, I die to the world and my soul is reincarnated in another body again and again. There is no escaping the island, there is no escaping reincarnation, and there is no escaping life. Only through ascension can we avoid reincarnation; only with the boat with no oar can we escape the island.

When the trees on the island are young, that denotes a young soul being born into the world, a new arrival into collective humanity. Welcome, young one. Make yourself at home. You will be here a while, and you'll have a lot to learn. But you will be ready someday perhaps in a thousand or so years when your soul is fully mature and ready.

The tree on the left is love and part of creation; the tree in the middle is agony, destruction, and negativity; the tree on the right is righteousness. Before ascension, the left eye, love, and the right eye, righteous, merge into one in the middle with destruction as the foundation. They form a complete, sacred triangle and launch straight up into the ether, into ascension. Conclusively, the boat with no oar is the sacred triangle.

God

When I was young, I had an audience with God. But before that, I had to pray every night before I went to sleep. I prayed for an audience with God night after night. I wanted to meet him and find out more about him.

One night, a goddess came and took me to see God. She was dressed like a traditional Middle Eastern woman in all black; only her face was visible. Being a goddess, she was beautiful; she resembled a European and a Persian. Maybe being properly dressed was part of the protocol when having an audience with God.

She somehow took me straight up through the ether and into the celestial temple, where I floated and glided down the long, great hall of the gods. The hallway was surprisingly dark considering where I was—in heaven. On each side of the hallway were niches that held religious symbols of the world's main religions. They glowed with a warm, white light and buzzed with the voices of all the people petitioning and praying to God.

At the end of the great hall was the throne room. I was told to wait. I saw a long flight of stairs supposedly ascending to a platform on which I expected to see a throne, but I saw only a platform with a big, pitch-black doorway in the background. Moments later, a throne emerged from the doorway and slid onto the platform.

On it sat an old man wearing a dark, royal robe. He looked European. He had a long, white beard. His right arm rested on the side of the throne. With his left hand, he held a long staff with an ornament on the top. He appeared ancient, royal, and important. He seemed to be a statue; he did not move. It was as if he were from another dimension, one of perfection and a perpetual state of ascension.

To his left was the beautiful goddess looking down on me. She was proud, elated. Her body language and her beautiful eyes were telling me, "Behold, the almighty God." As I gazed at this ancient being, something extraordinary happened. A psychic pulse rippled from him toward me and passed right through me. As that happened, a stentorian voice thundered and rumbled all around me—"I am your God!"

I trembled and shook in fear of the awesome power of the sound. I was in awe and at a loss. But part of me wondered if this being was for real or just some big scam or something luring me into submitting my will and belief. I naively asked, "Are you my god?" Instantly, the mood of the reception changed. The once-beautiful goddess's eyes and expression were showing signs of great discontent. I realized that this being before me was the real deal; my disrespect for God and my embarrassing the goddess who had arranged this holy meeting were serious matters. Before I had a chance to apologize for my childish behavior, I was booted out and sent back to earth, or to hell.

CHAPTER 3

The Nine-Step Dance of the Divine

According to the gods, my life path number is thirty-three, and so be it. For a number to truly embody a master number, it must have been ordained so by the gods. Otherwise, the number is reduced to a single digit. The master numbers are eleven, twenty-two, and thirty-three. These numbers represent angels in human forms, and they are the divine instruments on earth for assisting and helping humanity.

The master numbers are the angels who identify themselves by how many wings they have—master number eleven is an angel with two wings, master number twenty-two is an angel with four wings, and master number thirty-three is an angel with six wings. I am not a numerologist, but I am going some with this.

The Churning of the World Ocean of Milk at Angkor Wat in Cambodia

Around the twelfth century AD, something monumental and unprecedented in the history of humanity was being religiously and meticulously carved into the stone wall of a great temple, Angkor Wat. Miraculously, the carving remains intact. It had witnessed the rise and fall of many empires. It had seen humanity in its greatness. It had suffered the inhumanity humanity willed upon itself.

This carving was different from others in that it contained hidden messages from an ancient legend about the true meanings and purposes of human progress. When humanity is ready for peace, the ancient carving will reveal itself and unleash its hidden secrets and treasures upon its people and the world. These treasures have been given to them by the gods long ago. Hindu monks decided that the gifts were too far advanced for their time and too dangerous for them to involve the ruling class in them, so they carved the messages into the stone of the great temple and enchanted it for the future.

It Begins

According to Hindu legend, during creations, there were two opposing forces, the *asuras* (demons) and the *devas* (gods). They fought for control of the universe. The battles went on forever back and forth; no one had the upper hand until one side made a mistake. The devas, being all good and pure, channeled their powers from that source of goodness and purity. To maintain that connection, the devas had to stay pure and free of vice and vanity or they would lose their connections and become weak.

Indra, the king of the devas, made a mistake when he indulged in vanity. He and the other devas had to pay a hefty price. They lost their connections to the source and were weakened. The asuras took advantage of this situation; they triumphed over the devas and took control of the universe. The devas suffered humiliation and defeat and went into exile.

The asuras ran the universe; they roamed freely and displayed arrogance and complacency thinking that the weakling devas would never again be a threat to them. But the devas took advantage of this opportunity and gathered the remnants of their forces. They appealed to Vishnu, the second in the triumvirate of the gods. They told him they wanted their powers back so they could control the universe.

Vishnu told the devas to stay put and be ready. He would devise a plan that involved the participation of the asuras and the devas. The tricky part was to get the asuras to go along with it, but Vishnu was persuasive. The asuras had no choice but to agree to a temporary cease-fire, a hiatus. They went along with the plan.

Vishnu explained to the asuras that during their past conflicts with the devas, much of creation had ended up in ruins. Among these ruins were many great treasures and the most pride treasure of all, the *amrita*, the elixir of immortality. To retrieve these treasures, the asuras and the devas had to learn to work with each other without killing each other. Thus, an unlikely and unholy alliance was formed.

Under the flag of truce, the asuras agreed that all

the treasures retrieved from the Ocean of Milk would be shared equally with the devas. But Vishnu knew that if the amrita appeared, the asuras would take it by force from the weakling devas. Unbeknown to the asuras, Vishnu was planning to turn on the asuras should that happen.

As the plan unfolded, a mountain was carved off into a giant churning rod and placed in the Ocean of Milk, the Ocean of Immortality. Vasuki, the king serpent Naga, volunteered to have his serpentine body wrapped around the giant rod and be used as a rope that could be pulled back and forth much like a tug-of-war game. The asuras claimed the head side of Vasuki while the devas had to be content with the tail.

But Vishnu informed the devas that the head of Vasuki was filled with poison and that the asuras would be weakened by it. As a result, the asuras had to work even harder.

Right from the start, the giant rod was starting to sink into the ocean. A giant tortoise, one of Vishnu's incarnations, helped stop the giant rod from sinking by using its shell to support the rod. Vishnu managed the operation in the middle and helped both sides. He kept an eye on the giant rod and the emerging lost treasures.

This arduous labor went on for thousands of years, but many precious things were recovered and were shared equally among the asuras and devas. Tensions were high on both sides as the anticipated amrita, the elixir of immortality, made its appearance.

The asuras made their move; they took the amrita for themselves. But Vishnu took back the amrita and gave it to the devas. The devas drank it and became powerful and immortal. One asura managed to take a drink of it, but before he could swallow it, Vishnu cut off his head, so only his head became immortal.

With their power and their immortality, the devas defeated the asuras and maintained their control of the universe.

The Chain Reactions Part 1

Conflicts and dramas have occurred on the cosmic scale and possibly in another dimension and different time and space, but the reverberations from the events affect all realities and worlds from the constellations down to molecules. All life forms, us included, are the result of that moment of divine transgression of the asuras and devas.

As carbon-based life forms, our bodies contain the essence of Vishnu, the preserver and maintainer of all. Vishnu, the carbon god, holds together the Churning of the World Ocean of Milk to extract the amrita, the elixir of immortality. He is depicted as the six-limbed god, the balancer in the carvings at Angkor Wat. The Hindu monks intentionally hid his right leg in the carving to show Vishnu as five-limbed god to depict him in the human DNA sequence structure as deoxyribose, five-carbon sugar molecules.

In the cosmos, Vishnu holds together the churning of the World Ocean of Milk to extract the amrita. In the human body, Vishnu as the deoxyribose holds together the DNA strands of molecules and pulls on both sides to achieve the human state of ascension—immortal existence.

The Mini Universe

Humans, mini universes, are also the progeny of the gods. When a mother gives birth to a child, she also gives birth to a universe. The mother is the creator, the nurturer, and the teacher of the young universe. She takes on the characteristics of a god to care for her child, a young universe.

During creation in the cosmos, it takes thousands of years for the Churning of the World Ocean of Milk to yield anything precious as well as the amrita. Thus, it takes thousands of years for a human soul to experience life as a human being and eventually evolve and achieve ascension. The scenarios are one and the same; each one of us is unique, a mini universe. The divine struggles and the fights in the cosmos long ago between the asuras and the devas are being reenacted in each of us, mini universes.

No one knows the engineer of human DNA and how it arranges itself so ornately and elegantly; the matter has mystified the scientific community for almost a century. When the gods said they had created the universe, this is what they meant. Their essences are coursing through our veins and manifesting themselves in our DNA strands. If anyone is still looking for proof of the existence of the gods, this is it. The tricky part is finding ways to make human DNA respond to us first. This requires joint participation between science and mysticism. The two must put aside their differences and learn how to work together to establish this first contact between humanity and divinity.

The Chain Reactions Part 2—Eighty-Eight Asuras vs. Eighty-Eight Devas and the Origin of Numerology

One carving at Angkor Wat depicts the ancient Hindu legend about the Churning of the World Ocean of Milk. It portrays the asuras (titans) and the devas (gods) engaging in what looks like a tug of war; they are pulling on the snake king, Vasuki. But truth to be told, there have been tugs of war from the beginning.

Before starting on a long and arduous journey of going nowhere, being locked in place for thousands of years, Vishnu had a plan. As director of operations, he wanted to gauge the strengths and weaknesses of both sides and the number of steps required for the full effects of the rod's turning. He started out with equal numbers of asuras and devas, eighty-eight each, pulling on either end of the snake in opposite directions.

The asuras, weakened by the poison of Vasuki, yielded the first step to the devas. Realizing this weakness, Vishnu increased the rank of demons by one. The asuras yielded another step to the devas, so a second demon was added to their ranks. This happened one more time, but then, the strength remained even on both sides. Realizing this, Vishnu stopped adding demons, and he noticed that the steps would be in favor of the devas because the momentum from the turning of the giant rod kept it going in the direction of the devas. But it gradually slowed down. It came to a stop after the ninth step, also completing a full-turning cycle of the giant rod.

Vishnu declared from that point on that there would be ninety-one asuras on one side and eighty-eight devas on the other and that each side would take turn to pull after completing the nine-step cycle.

A numerology of ten numbers was born, zero being the first number. It is the point of beginning, and it represents the zero point where there is no activity on either side. The asuras and the devas do not move. Therefore, it never materializes in the physical world.

The physical numbers are numbers one through four. One, being the second number, represents the first step and the first victory by the gods over the demons. Forceful and furiously fast, the number didn't have time to form itself in anything but a straight line.

Two, the third number, represents changes in momentum and a realization of duality. When a demon is added to the ranks, it causes the momentum of the gods to slow down long enough for the number to take shape but incompletely. To fulfill this deficiency, two is forever searching for a companion.

Three, the fourth number, represents the completion of changes continuing from number two. It expresses itself without thinking. It's a number filled with curiosity and a sense of adventure. It lacks identity, and it seeks itself through the arts and expression.

Four, the fifth number and the last of the physical numbers, represents the final change in the physical and the final act of Vishnu adding a demon to the ranks. It lacks curvature and fluidity; it is a rigid number. Turning skyward, four receives messages and ideas from heaven and materializes them in the physical world.

Five, the neutral and the sixth number, represents balance in the physical world. The demons and gods are of equal strength, but momentum keeps turning in the gods' favor. Five represents the mastery of the physical but is still rigid in the intellect. However, should five put some effort into higher learning and abstaining from indulging itself, it has a greater chance than the other numbers do to attain perfection and eventually ascension. As is the case with number one, five's shape has openings and is connected on both sides. They are the most open-minded numbers in numerology.

The sacrificial numbers six through nine carry the burden of responsibilities in numerology. Six represents the first in higher thinking, empathy, and momentum. The demons and gods are deadlocked; only the momentum of the gods keeps the giant rod turning in their favor. This momentum gives rise to higher thoughts and emotions. Six, the first of emotions and feelings, associates itself with love, nurturing, and tending to the needs of others before itself, the first sacrifice.

Seven, the eighth number, reflects the actions and experiences of the numbers up to seven. It collects the data from all the past numbers and changes them to words, contexts, theories, philosophies, and religions. Seven is a spiritual number and represents seeking enlightenment. To accomplish this, seven seeks a solitary existence. It is a loner, the second sacrifice.

Eight, the ninth number, represents the extreme in sacrifice. Chosen by destiny to lead humanity to a better world, eight is forged and hammered in the furnace of destiny from zero and into the infinite shapes of all things. Number-eight people are extreme and take on an incredible burden of responsibility. They have a sixth sense when it comes to success in business, and they are gold mines for their employers. Eight is our salvation and messiah in the business world. It is self-contained and self-reliant. From the beginning, eight is constantly tortured and tormented by destiny, the third sacrifice.

Nine, the tenth number, represents the end of the road. The higher thinking and empathy starting from number six is gradually slowing down to a complete stop at number nine. As the end of revolution, number nine is the grandfather, protector, mentor, and peacekeeper for all the other numbers. It is the fourth and last sacrifice.

Duality and Numbers

Duality is the world of two—right and wrong, day and night, up and down, black and white, good and evil. We live in this dimension. Our souls split in two when we enter this dimension. Even the divine forces are splitting into good and evil. Thus, the numbers are also not spared of this split dimension, this duality. These split numbers are mirror images of each other and are paired as follows: zero and eight, one and five, two and three, four and seven, and six and nine.

Zero and eight are the first pair. Destiny chooses zero to be forged and hammered in its furnace. In fact, zero is not from this physical universe. But after many years of torments by destiny, zero transforms itself into eight by bending and twisting itself into it. Nothing is in between; it is either zero or eight; it is either nothing or the infinity of all things. If zero cannot be bent into eight, it will remain a zero, a nothing.

One and five are the second pair. One comes out charging head-on so fast that it doesn't have time to form anything but a straight line. However, number five is content and satisfied; it is the completion, the refinement, of one.

Two and three constitute the third pair. Two lacks direction and is prone to hesitancy, so it is constantly searching for a companionship. Three is the completion of two, but it's unsure of itself and lacks identity.

Four and seven are the fourth pair. They are mirror images of each other. Both are antenna numbers—four points up to heaven for ideas and is a conduit to the beyond. Seven points to the past and learns from it.

Six and nine are the last pair. Six is the beginning of empathy and higher thinking. It is also the first sacrifice. Nine, the final number, is the graduation number. It is the last empathetic and higher-thinking number and is the last sacrificial number.

These pairs show similar characteristics, some more than others. This prompts further study of their origins and purposes. I am at my limit when it comes to making these concepts clearer. Despite all my attempts, I fear the opposite.

Types of Numbers

The kinetic numbers—one through four—are the explosive numbers of numerology. They are always on the move and never settle down in any one place for long. They are the movers and shakers of this world. They are first to cross the finish line, and they have little patience for sticking around and collecting their trophies.

But what they lack in grace and finesse they make up

for in speed and audacity. Reckless and fearless, they do need to take it down a notch or two and yield to the grand finale of moderation. They need to learn how slow down and take time to enjoy their successes and accomplishments. Otherwise, they're prone to physical injuries and ailments, and they die young.

The potential numbers—six through nine—are diligent, slow, and methodical, but nothing is hidden from them. They exist in the universe of the mind and imagination. They prefer to spend their days dreaming and imagining themselves far away or even nowhere at all. They are the masters of introspection and cognition.

But as extraordinary as they are, they are very lazy. They exhibit myriad forms of health problems including obesity. They are in dire need of using their motor skills and must participate regularly in activities such as exercising and playing sports. A healthy dose of good, balanced nutrition would help them.

Five, the balance number, is envied and emulated by all. According to Buddhist legend, before Siddhartha Gautama achieved nirvana, he had a vision of a god playing a three-stringed banjo. As he was sitting under the Bodhi Tree deep in meditation, he listened to the beautiful melodies coming from the banjo played by a god. The divine was trying to assist him in his enlightenment.

The music suddenly stopped, but then it started again. That time, however, only one string at a time was being plucked. The first string was too tight and made him felt uneasy and agitated. The third string was too loose and made him felt nauseous and bland. But the middle string was soothing to his ears. Not too tight and not too loose, it was a perfectly balanced string. He felt calm and at ease. Eureka! He had found the perfect tone he had been searching for, the middle way, the way of balance, the way of number five.

The numbers match the strings of the divine banjo. Numbers one through four belong to the first string, the string of high tension. Numbers six through nine are identified with the third string, the string of looser tension. Five is fitting itself harmoniously with the middle string, not too tight and not too loose—a perfectly balanced string.

The End Game

All humans have their purposes. If they serve their purposes, their souls are subject to recall and are reincarnated in new vessels with new purposes. But after thousands of years of reincarnating, some are ready for departing this plane of existence and being reborn in a different world or a different existence—the god existence.

From the moment we are born, we are categorized by the numbers one through nine; their personalities and behaviors coincide with their assigned numbers, their destiny numbers. Thus, to escape from this prison existence and into the ranks of the gods, humans must find the right mind-sets and conditions to have a better chance of ascending. Those whose numbers are not five must adjust and recondition themselves so they become in accord with the balanced number five. Those whose number is five have a better chance than most to achieve ascension.

What am I? I am the pope. I am the president of the people of the free world. I am an emperor of a great empire. I am king or queen of a great country. I am a general. I am the guru. I am a garbageman. I am a grandfather, a grandmother, a father, a mother, a brother, a sister, a cousin, a friend. I am everyone.

I may be regarded as a titan in this world, but inside, I am rotten to the core just as everybody else is from the pope to the garbageman. I am a monster pretending to be human. It makes no different who or what I am to you in this world. Do not revere or worship me because I am tainted and defiled. Like the carving of the Churning of the World Ocean of Milk, it is inside of me and everybody else. In part of my heart is a horde of demons. In another part of my heart is a desperate group of gods. They will engage in a tug of war for the amrita and my soul for thousands of years.

When I was a young soul, the demon side of me did not influence me much; it allowed me time to grow and mature. But after thousands of years lying dormant and sensing the imminent arrival of the amrita, the demons came out of their slumber and went to work trying to take control of my heart, mind, and soul. Without the amrita, the gods in me were vulnerable and mortal. For the moment, the demons were subdued by the poison from Vasuki's mouth. Otherwise, the demons in me would have had the upper hand and would have taken control of my entire self.

Yes, my mind and soul were teetering on the edge of madness. This fortunate turn of events allowed me time to maintain my cohesive thought and a semblance of morality. But should there be disturbances in my psyche such as physical or mental abuse and addictions, the balance would shift to favor the demons, the dark side. It's a matter of when.

This is a big problem in our today society. We cannot

drink excessively or indulge ourselves in other ways; we must be moderate. We cannot continue to abuse ourselves, our loved ones, or anyone else. That must stop here and now. By indulging in these bad habits, we knowingly and unknowingly aid our dark sides.

We need to experience this karmic journey to evolve our souls. We have had enough of excessive drinking and killing ourselves. Our societies have progressed to the point that we are ready to ascend and awaken to a new understanding, a new world without war, a world in which we coexist peacefully with all others.

If you are ready for awakening, you must become ready for ascension. The gods in you will make you immortal when you ascend if you subdue the dark forces in you. This has been the goal from the beginning. If you are not ready for ascension, you must accept the path of enlightenment. Maybe the next reincarnation is the one for you. Good luck!

I have spent agonizing months trying to decipher what is in my head and in my heart and turn it into words. Please enjoy my writing and embrace the knowledge in this book. Thank you.

Your friend,
Khamsone

ABOUT THE AUTHOR

Khamsone Limsavanh came to United States in the late of 1981 as refugee from Laos. He joined the US. Army infantry in 1992-1996 with a final rank of Specialist. After the Army, he went back home and back to college pursuing an electrical engineering degree, but with no success. After dropping out from college, he move to Florida. Spending 12 years in practicing meditation, he finally achieved ascension in 2006.

Although an ascended being, he is not an ascended master by any means. In the summer of 2017, the carving of The Churning of The World Ocean of Milk in Angkor Wat calls out to him and wants him to reveal its secrets to the world. He later learns he is a channeler with a latent-human-psychic ability.

The reason he joins the U.S. Army is because he wants to do his part of appreciating his adopted country, America, for what its done for him and for his people. This book is also part of his many contributions to America, a country he calls home.

Printed in the United States
By Bookmasters

Printed in the United States
By Bookmasters